Now Are We in
Christ
Jesus

KENNETH COPELAND

KENNETH
COPELAND
PUBLICATIONS

Unless otherwise noted, all scripture is from the *King James Version* of the Bible.

Now Are We in Christ Jesus

ISBN 0-938458-03-5   30-0015

08 07 06 05 04 03   22 21 20 19 18 17

© 1980 Eagle Mountain International Church, Incorporated aka Kenneth Copeland Ministries

Kenneth Copeland Publications
Fort Worth, Texas 76192-0001

For more information about Kenneth Copeland Ministries, call 1-800-600-7395 or visit www.kcm.org.

Now Are We in Christ Jesus

Cease not to give thanks for you, making mention of you in my prayers; That the God of our Lord Jesus Christ, the Father of glory, may give unto you the spirit of wisdom and revelation in the knowledge of him: The eyes of your understanding being enlightened; that ye may know what is the hope of his calling, and what the rights of the glory of his inheritance in the saints...For we are his workmanship, created in Christ Jesus unto good works, which God hath before ordained that we should walk in them. Wherefore remember, that ye being in time past

Gentiles in the flesh, who are called Uncircumcision by that which is called the Circumcision in the flesh made by hands; That at that time ye were without Christ, being aliens from the commonwealth of Israel, and strangers from the convenants of promise, having no hope, and without God in the world: But now in Christ Jesus ye who sometimes were far off are made nigh by the blood of Christ (Ephesians 1:16-18, 2:10-13).

When you made Jesus the Lord of your life, something happened to you. You were created in Christ Jesus. You were given an inheritance. Now, you are in Christ Jesus. You are born of God.

In the physical realm, you were born of your mother. You weren't created; you were born. But in the spiritual realm, when you were "born of God," you were re-created by God. A change took place. You were reborn. The Bible says in 2 Corinthians 5:17 that you became a new creature, a new creation. *"Therefore if any man be in Christ, he is a new creature: old things are passed away; behold, all things are become new."* One translation says that any man who is in Christ Jesus is "a new species of being that never existed before."

When you accepted Jesus as your Lord, an actual creation took place. The old man—your unregenerated spirit man—was replaced by a new man, created in Christ Jesus. Old things passed away and all things became new. The new birth that occurred in you was done by the creative power of God. It took place inside you—in your spirit.

The "creation" that occurs at the new birth is the same type of "creation" that took place in the first chapter of Genesis. The word translated *created* in Genesis 1:1 gives the impression that before God brought heaven and earth into existence, there was nothing like it anywhere else. The same is true with the "new creation in Christ Jesus." You are a "new species of being that never existed before."

Being in Christ

You are a complete and total individual. There has never been, and never will be, another person just like you. When you received Jesus as Lord, God brought you into existence by His creative power. You were born of the Spirit of God. A seed was sown in your heart—the incorruptible seed of

God's Word—and you were placed *in Christ Jesus.*

You need to know and understand the reality of being in Christ. It is an outstanding revelation from God's Word that will affect your thinking, your believing, your actions and your speech.

Ephesians 2:13 says, *"But now in Christ Jesus ye who sometimes were far off are made nigh by the blood of Christ."* When? NOW. When are you in Christ Jesus? The moment you make Jesus your Lord.

Who is in Christ Jesus? Ephesians 1:10 says, *"That in the dispensation of the fulness of times he might gather together in one all things in Christ, both which are in heaven, and which are on earth; even in him."* So it's not just those who have died and gone to heaven that are in Christ Jesus. This scripture says, *"all things in Christ, both which are in heaven, and which are on earth; even in him."* Verse 13 says, *"In whom ye also trusted, after that ye heard the word of truth, the gospel of your salvation: in whom also after that ye believed, ye were sealed with that holy Spirit of promise."*

The most effective way that I have found to develop the reality of being in Christ is to begin with the book of Romans and search through all the letters of the New Testament for the phrase, *in Christ.* For example, as we have read in 2 Corinthians 5:17, *"Therefore if any man be in Christ, he is a new creature."* Scriptures that refer to being "in Christ," "in Him" or "in whom" occur 134 times in the Bible. Find those scriptures and read them carefully. Study them and run cross-references on them. You can be sure that whatever the Word says about being "in Christ," it belongs to you because you are in Christ Jesus.

Being in Christ means that you are "the saved." Why? Because you have confessed with your mouth that Jesus is Lord and have believed in your heart that God raised Him from the dead (Romans 10:9).

Being in Christ means that you are "the healed." Why? Because Jesus went to the cross, bore the curse of the Law, and broke the power of sickness and disease. He was made sick with our sickness; but He didn't stay sick. Today, He is healed; and because we are in Him, we are healed, too!

Being in Christ means you are "the delivered." Why? Because Colossians 1:13 says God has delivered us from the power of darkness and has translated us into the kingdom of God's dear Son.

Jesus said he was sent to preach deliverance to the captives (Luke 4:18).

All of the power that it takes to save any human being, to heal any human being, to deliver any human being, came into this earth on the Day of Pentecost. When Jesus walked into a place, the power was there to heal the people. Why? Because the power was in Him. He said, *"The Father that dwelleth in me, he doeth the works"* (John 14:10). Now, that power is in you because you are in Him. Because you are in Christ Jesus, you can live like Him, talk like Him, and act like Him. The Word of God will change you— spirit, soul and body.

The Bible says that God sent Jesus that He might become the firstborn of many brethren (Romans 8:29). God planted the seed of His Son, Jesus, in order to get a harvest, and He reaps that harvest as new souls are added to the kingdom of God. The hundredfold principle is now in operation.

You are called a joint heir with Christ Jesus. The Word says that when you made Jesus your Lord, you became one spirit with Him. You are in Him. God sees you in Jesus. He not only came inside you, but you went inside Him. We have preached that Jesus comes inside a person, but we have thought very little of the fact that we have entered into Him. You are the Body of Christ. Jesus said, *"If ye abide in me, and my words abide in you, ye shall ask what ye will, and it shall be done unto you"* (John 15:7). You are abiding in Him.

Ephesians 1:4 says, *"According as he hath chosen us in him before the foundation of the world, that we should be holy and without blame before him in love."*

You are holy and without blame before Him in love. Jesus provided for you that God is your own Heavenly Father. You are no longer without hope and without God in the world (Ephesians 2:12). You have been accepted in the beloved (Ephesians 1:6). The letter that Paul wrote to the Ephesians was written to you as well because you are in Christ Jesus. It's a letter from God to you saying, "I have accepted you in My Son. You are in the Beloved. You are Mine."

Have you ever heard the phrase; "But I'm so unworthy"? That was true before you got saved. You were not worthy to receive what Jesus did. But He did it anyway! Because He died for you, you can live in Him. He made you worthy. You have been created in Christ Jesus and there is nothing unworthy in Him.

You are not worthy because of anything *you* did, but because of Jesus and what He did for you. Some people say, "Brother, I know we're in Christ Jesus, but I just can't stand up and say that I'm healed." None of us deserves it in and of ourselves, but God knew that. If you have sin in your life, get it out. If you can't receive healing from God because of the way you have been living, quit living that way! Repent and get rid of it! The Word says that God is faithful and just to forgive us of our sins when we confess them (1 John 1:9). When you confess the sin, He will forgive you. Don't rebel against God. Don't run *from* God when you sin, run *to* Him! If you have to rebel, then rebel against the devil, not God. The Bible says, *"Awake to righteousness, and sin not"* (1 Corinthians 15:34).

As a born-again believer, sin has no dominion over you. It can't dominate you. It has to leave you. Satan is a defeated foe; he is not your god. James 4:7 says that if you resist him, he will flee from you.

You need to see yourself "in Christ" and know the reality of it. If you ask some people today, "Are you a son of God?" They'll say, "Who, me? Certainly not!" When you ask, "Are you saved?" they'll say, "Oh yes, thank God, I'm just an old sinner, saved by grace." No, you are not! You *were* a sinner; you got saved by grace! You can't be both at once. You are a new creation in Christ Jesus. You have been born into the kingdom of His love. As far as God is concerned, you are holy, blameless, and beyond reproach. So quit thinking, speaking, and acting like the world. Let go of all those religious "sin tags."

Begin confessing that you are the righteousness of God in Christ.

Your Inheritance

What does it mean to obtain an inheritance? Acts 20:32 says, *"And now, brethren, I commend you to God, and to the word of his grace, which is able to build you up, and to give you an inheritance among all them which are sanctified."* The Word is what will build you up and give you your inheritance.

Ephesians 1:11 says, **"In whom also we have obtained an inheritance, being predestinated according to the purpose of him who worketh all things after the counsel of his own will."** This doesn't say you are going to obtain your inheritance; it says you have already obtained it. This verse of scripture is past tense. You *have obtained* an inheritance. You *have been accepted* in the beloved. Part of your inheritance includes your family position with God in heaven after you lay down your body, but you have entered into your inheritance in Him right now here on this earth. You have the right to operate in that inheritance today.

Colossians 1:12 says, *"Giving thanks unto the Father, which hath made us meet to be partakers of the inheritance of the saints in light."* The word meet is an Old English word that means able. God has made you able to be a partaker of the inheritance of the saints in light. Verses 13-14 say, *"Who hath delivered us from the power of darkness, and hath translated us into the kingdom of his dear Son: In whom we have redemption through his blood."* You are "the redeemed." Jesus has made you able to be a partaker of that inheritance. It's yours! You are able to receive it and walk in it because God has said you are able. A literal translation of verse 12 is, "Who has made us able to enjoy our share of the inheritance." You are to give thanks unto the Father, Who has made you able to enjoy your share of the inheritance. So thank God for it! Praise and thanksgiving unto the Father play a big part in receiving your inheritance.

What did you inherit in Him? Did you just inherit heaven as your home? No. Hebrews 1:4 says, *"Being made so much better than the angels as he hath by inheritance obtained a more excellent name than they."* You have inherited Jesus' authority as well as His Name. You have inherited the kingdom of God. Colossians 2:9-10 says, *"For in him dwelleth all the fulness of the Godhead bodily. And ye are complete in him,*

17

which is the head of all principality and power." There is embodied in you all that is in the Godhead—Jesus, the Spirit of God, the Heavenly Father, the mind of Christ, the faith of God, the love of God. You have in you the very life of God, because you are in Christ Jesus.

Everything Jesus received when He was raised from the dead, everything that has happened to Jesus since He was raised from the dead, is yours—not just part of it, all of it!

When Jesus was raised from the dead, He received a glorified body. You will get one, too.

Where did Jesus go when He was raised? To the right hand of the Father. That's where you are now! Ephesians 2:6 says, *"And hath raised us up together, and made us sit together in heavenly places in Christ Jesus."* Jesus was raised from the dead by the mighty power of God and was seated at His own right hand in the heavenly places. That same mighty power of God worked in you when you made Jesus the Lord of your life. It raised you up and set you in heavenly places in Christ Jesus.

He is in you and you are in Him. *His inheritance and your inheritance are one and the same.* You are a joint heir with Him.

The Apostle Paul prayed that the eyes of our understanding be enlightened to know the glory of our inheritance in the saints and the exceeding greatness of God's power toward us who believe (Ephesians 1:18-19).

The exceeding greatness of His power. What does His power mean to the believer? Let's read on in Ephesians 1:20-23:

Which he wrought in Christ, when he raised him from the dead, and set him at his own right hand in the heavenly places, Far above all principality, and power, and might, and dominion, and every name that is named, not only in this world, but also in that which is to come: And hath put all things under his feet, and gave him to be the head over all things to the church, Which is his body, the fulness of him that filleth all in all.

The Body of Christ is "the fullness of Him." He is not full and complete without you and you are not full and complete without Him.

Colossians 1:21-23 says, *"And you...hath he reconciled In the body of his flesh through death, to present you holy and unblameable and unreprove-able in his sight: If ye continue in the faith grounded and settled, and be not moved away from the hope of the gospel, which ye have heard.*" Don't be moved away from the gospel. Don't be moved away from the things the Word is telling you. Don't think: *That couldn't be for me.* Don't allow the devil or anyone else to move you away from the inheritance that rightfully belongs to you in Christ Jesus. When the Word says that you are holy, unblameable and unreproveable in the sight of God, then receive it.

We see from God's Word that *in Him* you are holy and without blame before God. Philippians 2:15 says, "*That ye may be blameless and harmless, the sons of God, without rebuke, in the midst of a crooked and perverse nation, among whom ye shine as lights in the world.*" We shine as lights. Where? *In the world.*

You are in the Body of Christ here on earth. If you are in His Body, then you are in Him. You are His workmanship, created in Christ Jesus. In the eyes of God you are holy and blameless, beyond reproach and without rebuke. You, as a believer, are to hold forth the Word of life in the midst of a crooked and perverse generation.

If you have a working revelation of your redemption in Christ Jesus, there is not one prayer that needs to go unanswered or any need that has to go unmet. When you see that your inheritance contains a complete redemption from the curse of the Law, you will want to close the door to Satan and to the things of this world. You are redeemed from the curse, so don't allow it to operate in your affairs.

Isaiah 54:17 says, *"no weapon that is formed against thee shall prosper; and every tongue that shall rise against thee in judgement thou shalt condemn. This is the heritage of the servants of the Lord, and their righteousness is of me, saith the Lord."* Your righteousness is of the Lord. You need to see yourself in Him. See yourself the way the Word says you are, not how you are going to be.

John said, *"Beloved, now are we the sons of God"* (1 John 3:2). When? NOW! Paul wrote in Galatians 4:7, *"Wherefore thou art no more a servant, but a son; and if a son, then an heir of God through Christ."*

God's Word has the capacity and the power to give you an inheritance. Ephesians 1:3 says, *"Blessed be the God and Father of our Lord Jesus Christ, who hath blessed us with all spiritual blessings in heavenly places in Christ."* God has already unleashed in your life all the blessings that heaven has to offer. They are already yours! But God won't force them on you. You have to accept your inheritance in Christ Jesus and allow it to be a part of your life before you will be able to walk in it.

Living in Righteousness

Therefore if any man be in Christ, he is a new creature: old things are passed away; behold all things are become new. And all things are of God, who hath reconciled us to himself by Jesus Christ, and hath given to us the ministry of reconciliation; to wit, (or to know) that God was in Christ, reconciling the world unto himself, not imputing their trespasses unto them; and hath committed unto us the word of reconciliation...For he (God) hath made him (Jesus) to be sin for us, who knew no sin; that we might

be made the righteousness of God in him (2 Corinthians 5:17-21).

Being in Christ Jesus makes you a new creature, or a new creation. The literal Greek text says *a new species of being which never existed before.* When you become a new creature, your spirit is completely re-created. Old things are passed away, all things become new, and all things are of God. You need to realize that you are not a spiritual schizophrenic—half-God and half-Satan—you are all-God. The problem area is not in your spirit; it lies in your mind and body. It is every believer's responsibility to take God's Word and renew his mind, then he can use that Word to control his body. Look at Ephesians 4:20-24:

But ye have not so learned Christ; If so be that ye have heard him, and have been taught by

him, as the truth in Jesus: That ye put off concerning the former conversation the old man, which is corrupt according to the deceitful lusts; And be renewed in the spirit of your mind; And that ye put on the new man, which after God is created in righteousness and true holiness.

In Paul's letter to the Ephesian church, he was explaining to them that they had been delivered from their sinful flesh and had been re-created in righteousness. However, it was their responsibility as an act of their will to put on the new man in Christ and stop the works of the flesh. The same principle applies to you and me as believers today. We have been re-created by God in the spirit, but we must take the Word of God and use it to renew our minds and control our flesh.

Just knowing that you have been made the righteousness of God in Christ is not enough. You need to have a full understanding of what righteousness is and what it means to you as an individual believer. Many sincere Christians are living far below their privileges in Christ simply because they do not understand their place as a child of God. Righteousness is one of the most vital areas in the Christian walk. Without a knowledge of righteousness, you will never obtain all that is yours in God.

The word translated *righteousness* literally means *to be in right-standing*. When a person receives Jesus as Lord of his life, he is made righteous. By being brought into right-standing with God, every believer is given certain privileges or rights as God's child.

Some people confuse righteousness with holiness, but righteousness has nothing to do with the way you act. Holiness is your conduct; righteousness is what you are—the nature of God. You didn't come into right-standing with God by being good or acting right. It was faith in Jesus Christ and His redemptive work at Calvary that brought you into right-standing with God.

Your position in the Body of Christ can be compared to your position as a citizen of the United States. As an American citizen, you have certain rights that are outlined in the Constitution. These rights are called "The Bill of Rights." Had our forefathers been using Old English terminology, they would have called it, "The Bill of Righteousness." As long as you obey the laws of the land, you are a citizen in right-standing with the United States government.

These same principles apply to you as a child of God. Being a believer (being in Christ Jesus) makes you a citizen in the kingdom of God and entitles you to everything in that kingdom. The Bible is your spiritual "bill of righteousness," outlining all the rights and privileges available to you; whether or not you partake of your rights is another matter. Ignorance will rob you of the abundant life that is freely available to you.

The best illustration of this is the story of the man who saved for years to be able to buy a boat ticket to America. Once he had saved enough, he bought his ticket and boarded the ship. Since he didn't have any money left for food, he brought along some crackers and cheese. Every evening at mealtime, he would look into the dining room at the other passengers enjoying their food, then he would return to his cabin and eat his crackers and cheese. The day the ship docked in New York harbor, a steward came to him and said, "Sir, have we offended you in any way? I noticed that you didn't eat any of your meals in our dining room." The man answered, "Oh, no! You see, I didn't have enough money for meals so I ate in my room." Then the steward said, "But sir, your meals were included in the ticket!"

As Christians, we have an abundance of privileges available to us. They were bought and paid for by Jesus at Calvary. But if we don't know it, how can we take advantage of them?

In Ephesians 6:10-18, the Apostle Paul is describing the armor of God. *One of the most important pieces of this armor is the breastplate of righteousness.* A breastplate covers the vital parts of a soldier's body. Your right-standing with God acts as that breastplate. It covers the vital part of a Christian's identity—his right to the authority provided for him in Jesus Christ. You need to put on your breastplate of righteousness and wear it victoriously. It will bring the force of righteousness into operation on your behalf.

One of your rights in the kingdom is answered prayer. According to 1 Peter 3:12, *The eyes of the Lord are over the righteous, and his ears are open unto their prayers.* James 5:16 says, *The effectual fervent prayer of a right-eous man availeth much.* When you pray in faith, you have a right to expect your Heavenly Father to answer.

Developing what I call a "righteousness consciousness" will cause you to live an overcoming, victorious life. Jesus was in right-standing with the

Father during His earthwalk and the results He obtained were outstanding. As a child of God and joint heir with Jesus, you should expect to receive the same results. Jesus Himself said, *"He that believeth on me, the works that I do shall he do also; and greater works than these shall he do; because I go unto my Father"* (John 14:12).

Spend time in God's Word and find out for yourself the rights you have. When you do, righteousness will become an active, powerful force in your life.

Standing in a Point of Authority

One of the hardest things for people to understand and receive is living from a point of authority.

When you made Jesus the Lord of your life, Colossians 1:13 says you were delivered from the power of darkness. The word *power* is literally translated *authority*. You have been delivered from the power, or authority, of darkness and placed into God's kingdom. The kingdom of God includes both heaven and earth. Jesus said, *"All power is given unto me in heaven and in earth. Go ye therefore"* (Matthew 28:18-19.) That power was given to you as part of your inheritance in Christ Jesus. You have entered into this position of authority because you are in Him.

The Word says that righteousness has come upon all men (Romans 5:18). You may ask, "Then why don't all men become righteous?" Because in order to receive it, you have to act on righteousness from the point of authority.

On November 2, 1962, I used my authority as a human being and made a choice. I made the decision to receive

Jesus as Lord of my life. At that moment, the righteousness that had been upon me came inside me. I was *made* the righteousness of God in Christ. Second Corinthians 5:21 says, *"He hath made him to be sin for us, who knew not sin; that we might be made the righteousness of God in him."*

Because you have made Jesus your Lord, the new birth is now a reality in your spirit. You have been made the righteousness of God in Him. God wants to treat you like that. He wants to treat you as if you had never sinned. He sent Jesus to the cross to bear your sin, to completely wash away the sin that had been in you. Because you are in Jesus, God sees you the same way He sees Jesus. He wants to treat you like He treats Jesus—so let Him!

God's power is in His Word. He is upholding all things by the word of His power (Hebrews 1:3). You need to learn to minister and walk from a point of authority. In His earthwalk, Jesus said such things as *"Be thou made whole. Take up your bed and walk."* Then to a lame man Peter said in Acts 3:6, *"In the name of Jesus Christ of Nazareth rise up and walk."* He, too, ministered and spoke from a point of authority.

It's time for you as a believer to begin to act that way. You have obtained an inheritance, and in that inheritance you have been given all authority. The God of the universe lives inside you! He lives and walks in you. Become God-inside-minded and you will begin to walk in this point of authority.

Keep right on building yourself up in your inheritance. You live in a world that is full of evil influences. Satan wants to see to it that you forget the reality of being born again. When you see in the

Word that you are in Christ Jesus, that you are in Him, then confess it with all of your heart. Then you will be strong, standing in a point of authority and operating in your inheritance in Him.

Let This Mind Be in You

Philippians 2:5-6 says, *"Let this mind be in you, which was also in Christ Jesus: Who, being in the form of God, thought it not robbery to be equal with God."* You are to think the way Jesus thought. He didn't think it robbery to be equal with God.

Then verse 8 says, *"He humbled himself, and became obedient unto death, even the death of the cross."* You have to humble yourself. No one else can humble you. You are to humble yourself under the mighty hand of God, and at the same time, keep in mind that you are a joint heir with Jesus (1 Peter 5:6, Romans 8:17).

Kings and Priests

According to Romans 8:29, Jesus is *"the firstborn among many brethren."* Glory to God! Jesus is no longer *the only begotten* Son of God. Revelation 1:5-6 describes Jesus as *"the prince of the kings of the earth. Unto him that loved us, and washed us from our sins in his own blood, And hath made us kings and priests unto God and his Father; to him be glory and dominion for ever and ever."* You have been made a king and a priest unto God because of Jesus and the inheritance that He provided for you.

From the book of Acts to the Revelation of John, Jesus is known as *the first begotten from the dead.* If there is a firstborn, then there has to be a secondborn, a thirdborn, a fourth-born, etc. Every believer is counted as a child of God. We are members of God's family and heirs to all He has.

Jesus has made you a king and a priest. He has made you the righteous-ness of God in Him. In Him, you are *the accepted*. In Him, you are *the beloved*. You are His chosen and His elect—a royal priesthood that has been bought with His blood and made His own child.

First John 4:17 says, *"Herein is our love made perfect, that we may have boldness in the day of judgement: because as he is, so are we in this world."* As He is, so are *you* in this world! Because you have accepted the sacrifice of Jesus at Calvary and received Him as your Lord, you have the power and the authority to walk in the inheritance that He made available to you. But if you don't know what is yours and what belongs to you, you won't be able to enjoy the benefits of it. Find out what is included in your inheritance in Christ Jesus and then resist any influence that would try to convince you otherwise.

Luke 12:31-32 says, *"But rather seek ye the kingdom of God; and all these things shall be added unto you. Fear not, little flock; for it is your Father's good pleasure to give you the kingdom."* It is God's will to give you the kingdom, the whole kingdom! When the reality gets down in your heart that you are an heir of Almighty God, that He has given you the whole kingdom and has instructed you to seek first that kingdom, then all the benefits of your inheritance will be added unto you and you will grow and develop in God's Word.

However, you will never receive any portion of your inheritance until you begin to acknowledge it. With your thoughts, your words and your actions, you acknowledge the fact that you are in Christ Jesus, that you have received an inheritance, that you have the right to walk in all the blessings and promises of God's Word. Acknowledge the things of God and allow the assurance of them to enter into your heart. Then see them become a part of your life in every area.

How have you been approaching God...on the level of a king or on the level of a beggar? Are you backing your way into the presence of God, hoping to get a handout?

When you made Jesus your Lord, He made you able to stand in the presence of the Father God as a king and a priest, not as a beggar—as the righteousness of God in Christ, not as a sinner. You have been redeemed out of the kingdom of darkness and translated into the kingdom of God's dear Son. You have been redeemed into kingship and priesthood. You are a king and a priest in Christ Jesus!

Prayer for Salvation and Baptism in the Holy Spirit

Heavenly Father, I come to You in the Name of Jesus. Your Word says, "Whosoever shall call on the name of the Lord shall be saved" (Acts 2:21). I am calling on You. I pray and ask Jesus to come into my heart and be Lord over my life according to Romans 10:9-10. "If thou shalt confess with thy mouth the Lord Jesus, and shalt believe in thine heart that God hath raised him from the dead, thou shalt be saved. For with the heart man believeth unto right-eousness; and with the mouth confession is made unto salvation." I do that now. I confess that Jesus is Lord, and I believe in my heart that God raised Him from the dead.

I am now reborn! I am a Christian— a child of Almighty God! I am saved! You also said in Your Word, "If ye then, being evil, know how to give good gifts unto your children: HOW MUCH MORE shall your heavenly Father give the Holy Spirit to them that ask him?" (Luke 11:13). I'm also ask-ing You to fill me with the Holy Spirit. Holy Spirit, rise up within me as I praise God. I fully expect to speak with other tongues as You give me the utterance (Acts 2:4). In Jesus' Name. Amen!

Begin to praise God for filling you with the Holy Spirit. Speak those words and syllables you receive—not in your own language, but the language given to you by the Holy Spirit. You have to use your own voice. God will not force you to speak. Don't be concerned with how it sounds. It is a heavenly language!

Continue with the blessing God has given you and pray in the spirit every day.

You are a born-again, Spirit-filled believer. You'll never be the same!

Find a good church that boldly preaches God's Word and obeys it. Become a part of a church family who will love and care for you as you love and care for them.

We need to be connected to each other. It increases our strength in God. It's God's plan for us.

Make it a habit to watch the *Believer's Voice of Victory* television broadcast and become a doer of the Word who is blessed by his doing (James 1:22-25).

About the Author

Kenneth Copeland is co-founder and president of Kenneth Copeland Ministries in Fort Worth, Texas, and best-selling author of books that include *Managing God's Mutual Funds—Yours and His, How to Discipline Your Flesh* and *Honor—Walking in Honesty, Truth and Integrity.*

Now in his 36th year as a minister of the gospel of Christ and teacher of God's Word, Kenneth is the recording artist of such award-winning albums as his Grammy nominated *Only the Redeemed, In His Presence, He Is Jehovah* and his most recently released *Just a Closer Walk.* He also co-stars as the character Wichita Slim in the children's adventure videos *The Gunslinger, Covenant Rider* and the movie *The Treasure of Eagle Mountain,* and as Daniel Lyon in the *Commander Kellie and the Superkids$_{SM}$* videos *Armor of Light* and *Judgment: The Trial of Commander Kellie.*

With the help of offices and staff in the United States, Canada, England, Australia, South Africa and Ukraine, Kenneth is fulfilling his vision to boldly preach the uncompromised Word of God from the top of this world, to the bottom, and all the way around. His ministry reaches millions of people worldwide through daily and Sunday TV broadcasts, magazines, teaching tapes and videos, conventions and campaigns, and the World Wide Web.

Learn more about
Kenneth Copeland Ministries
by visiting our Web site at
www.kcm.org

Books Available From
Kenneth Copeland Ministries

by Kenneth Copeland

* * A Ceremony of Marriage
* A Matter of Choice
* Covenant of Blood
* Faith and Patience—The Power Twins
* * Freedom From Fear
* Giving and Receiving
* Honor—Walking in Honesty, Truth and Integrity
* How to Conquer Strife
* How to Discipline Your Flesh
* How to Receive Communion
* In Love There Is No Fear
* Know Your Enemy
* Living at the End of Time—A Time of
    Supernatural Increase
* Love Never Fails
* Managing God's Mutual Funds—Yours and His
* Mercy—The Divine Rescue of the Human Race
* * Now Are We in Christ Jesus
* One Nation Under God (gift book with CD enclosed)
* * Our Covenant With God
* Partnership, Sharing the Vision—Sharing the Grace
* * Prayer—Your Foundation for Success
* * Prosperity: The Choice Is Yours
* Rumors of War
* * Sensitivity of Heart
* * Six Steps to Excellence in Ministry
* * Sorrow Not! Winning Over Grief and Sorrow
* * The Decision Is Yours

*Available in Spanish

by Gloria Copeland

Books Co-Authored by Kenneth and Gloria Copeland

*Available in Spanish

One Word From God Can Change Your Life

One Word From God Series:
- One Word From God Can Change Your Destiny
- One Word From God Can Change Your Family
- One Word From God Can Change Your Finances
- One Word From God Can Change
    Your Formula for Success
- One Word From God Can Change Your Health
- One Word From God Can Change Your Nation
- One Word From God Can Change Your Prayer Life
- One Word From God Can Change Your Relationships

Load Up—A Youth Devotional
Over the Edge—A Youth Devotional
Pursuit of His Presence—A Daily Devotional
Pursuit of His Presence—A Perpetual Calendar

Other Books Published by KCP

The First 30 Years—A Journey of Faith
    The story of the lives of Kenneth and Gloria Copeland
Real People. Real Needs. Real Victories.
    A book of testimonies to encourage your faith
John G. Lake—His Life, His Sermons,
    His Boldness of Faith
The Holiest of All by Andrew Murray
The New Testament in Modern Speech
    by Richard Francis Weymouth
The Rabbi From Burbank by Rabbi Isidor Zwirn
    and Bob Owen
Unchained by Mac Gober

Products Designed for Today's Children and Youth

And Jesus Healed Them All (confession book and CD gift package)
Baby Praise Board Book
Baby Praise Christmas Board Book
Noah's Ark Coloring Book
The Best of *Shout!* Adventure Comics
The *Shout!* Giant Flip Coloring Book
The *Shout!* Joke Book
The *Shout!* Super-Activity Book
Wichita Slim's Campfire Stories

*Commander Kellie and the Superkids*_{SM} Books:

The SWORD Adventure Book
*Commander Kellie and the Superkids*_{SM}
   Solve-It-Yourself Mysteries
*Commander Kellie and the Superkids*_{SM}
   Adventure Series: Middle Grade Novels
   by Christopher P.N. Maselli:

#1 The Mysterious Presence
#2 The Quest for the Second Half
#3 Escape From Jungle Island
#4 In Pursuit of the Enemy
#5 Caged Rivalry
#6 Mystery of the Missing Junk
#7 Out of Breath
#8 The Year Mashela Stole Christmas

World Offices of
Kenneth Copeland Ministries

For more information about KCM and a free
catalog, please write the office nearest you:

Kenneth Copeland Ministries
Fort Worth, Texas 76192-0001

Kenneth Copeland
Locked Bag 2600
Mansfield Delivery Centre
QUEENSLAND 4122
AUSTRALIA

Kenneth Copeland
Post Office Box 15
BATH
BA1 3XN
U.K.

Kenneth Copeland
Private Bag X 909
FONTAINEBLEAU
2032
REPUBLIC OF
SOUTH AFRICA

Kenneth Copeland
Post Office Box 378
Surrey, B.C.
V3T 5B6
CANADA

Kenneth Copeland Ministries
Post Office Box 84
L'VIV 79000
UKRAINE

We're Here for You!

Believer's Voice of Victory Television Broadcast

Join Kenneth and Gloria Copeland and the *Believer's Voice of Victory* broadcasts Monday through Friday and on Sunday each week, and learn how faith in God's Word can take your life from ordinary to extraordinary. This teaching from God's Word is designed to get you where you want to be—*on top!*

You can catch the *Believer's Voice of Victory* broadcast on your local, cable or satellite channels.

Check your local listings for times and stations in your area.

Believer's Voice of Victory Magazine

Enjoy inspired teaching and encouragement from Kenneth and Gloria Copeland and guest ministers each month in the *Believer's Voice of Victory* magazine. Also included are real-life testimonies of God's miraculous power and divine intervention in the lives of people just like you!

It's more than just a magazine—it's a ministry.

Shout! The Voice of Victory for Kids

Shout!...The dynamic magazine just for kids is a Bible-charged, action-packed, quarterly magazine available FREE to kids everywhere! Featuring *Wichita Slim* and *Commander Kellie and the Superkids*_{SM}, *Shout!* is filled with colorful adventure comics, challenging games and puzzles, exciting short stories, solve-it-yourself mysteries and much more!!

Stand up, sign up and get ready to *Shout!*

To receive a FREE subscription to *Believer's Voice of Victory,* or to give a child you know a FREE subscription to *Shout!,* write to:

Kenneth Copeland Ministries
Fort Worth, Texas 76192-0001
Or call:
1-800-600-7395
(7 a.m.-5 p.m. CT)
Or visit our Web site at:
www.kcm.org

If you are writing from outside the U.S., please contact the KCM office nearest you. Addresses for all Kenneth Copeland Ministries offices are listed on the previous pages.